A **Fast-Start Guide** to
WARBURTON'S
Winning
S Y S T E M

*Tapping and Other Transformational
Mental Training Tools for Athletes*

**GREG
WARBURTON**

DENVER, COLORADO

A Fast-Start Guide to Warburton's Winning System:
Tapping and Other Transformational Mental Training Tools for Athletes
All Rights Reserved.
Copyright © 2013 Greg Warburton
v4.0

Outskirts Press, Inc.
http://www.outskirtspress.com

ISBN: 978-1-4787-0882-7

Outskirts Press and the "OP" logo are trademarks belonging to Outskirts Press, Inc.

PRINTED IN THE UNITED STATES OF AMERICA

Note to Reader:

Many of the names in this book have been changed to protect the identity of the player or client. In other cases, I have obtained permission to share the person's experience. In all cases, the experiences are reported as I observed them.

You can apply the techniques to any sport and customize the language and the system so that it works for you in your sport.

Contents

Introduction

THIS FAST-START GUIDE is a companion to my book, ***Warburton's Winning System: Tapping and Other Transformational Mental Training Tools for Athletes***. You can start building a stronger mental game right now by practicing the steps and using the techniques in this guide. You can apply this winning system to any sport. Feel free to customize the techniques and the language so they work for you and your sport.

No more days or weeks of agonizing over poor-performance moments. No more just suffering through slumps! As you diligently practice and ultimately master this system, the down times will no longer have the same grip on you. You will become self-confident and self-reliant. You will know what you can do to quickly and dependably flush bad-performance moments out of your mind and body.

If you study sports champions, you will discover that mastering mental training is the added action they take. Former Olympic champion Lanny Bassham says in his book, *With Winning in Mind,* "The only thing that separates the winners from the others is the way they think. Winners are convinced they will finish first..." Bassham also tells about asking another Olympic champion why he was so certain he would win gold again, and the champion responded, "I am more committed to mental training than any of my competitors!"

Develop an attitude of mastery. You already do this by diligently practicing your physical skills, now decide to develop, practice, and stick with your own mental-training system.

REMEMBER: CHAMPIONS DO WILLINGLY WHAT OTHERS WON'T DO AT ALL!

Do you start game-time feeling nervous and anxious?

Are you struggling to perform consistently at your best?

Have you ever worked really hard to analyze what's wrong when you aren't playing up to your potential?

Have you ever wondered how to break through mental blocks and stop pressing during game time? You know it's important, but you don't know how to do it?

Have you ever decided to be mentally tougher and, in the next moment, asked yourself, "But how do I get started?"

Do you know what the starting place is to build a consistently strong mental game?

The Foundation for a Strong Mental Game: Practice Self-Honesty

START BY TELLING yourself the truth. Self-honesty is a courageous act that leads to awareness about your habits and enables you to make the lasting changes you desire.

To practice self-honesty and trigger change in any area of your life, start by saying, *When I tell myself the truth,* I am thinking _____ and feeling _____ about my current athletic performance.

I call this practice self-honest self-observation, and it is the first step on the road to mastering your mental and emotional training. Learn to watch one thought/feeling at a time *without judging or getting mad at yourself.* Let's begin.

Step-By-Step

- Tell yourself the truth about what thoughts and feelings you are experiencing.
- Start watching your thinking and feeling experiences—one at a time.
- Watch your thoughts and feelings **without judging or getting mad at yourself**. Your job is to become aware. After diligently practicing this step, a college baseball player once told me: *I had been thinking I was a positive person, and then **I became aware** of how negative I was*. With awareness you can really make changes.
- Master the art of self-honest self-observation. Anything that happens in your life starts with your thought and feeling experiences. As you practice paying attention to these experiences, it will become natural and you will be able to quickly identify any trouble spots.

STEP 2: POSE AN EVALUATION QUESTION

- Ask one simple question about each thought or feeling you notice: *Will this thought and/or feeling work for me or against me in achieving the performance I want?*
  After testing this step, one of my students made the following comment: "Learning to ask myself the right questions is imperative in changing my direction…Will this _____ work for me or against me? How simple is that?"

STEP 3: STAY IN THE *DO* ZONE!

- Choose to make a mental shift if your answer to the question in Step 2 tells you that the thought or feeling will work against you.
- Decide to stop focusing on what you don't want to keep doing and put your mind on the performance you *do* want. For example: Instead of thinking/saying *Don't hook this drive*, reframe it to **I effortlessly drive the golf ball to my target area**. Or change your mental focus from *Don't take a called third strike* to **I see the ball clearly with two strikes.** Or change your mental focus from *I'm hitting the ball hard, but right at people* to **I consistently drive the ball into the gaps!**

STEP 4: CHOOSE A
POSITIVE-PERFORMANCE PHRASE

- Choose your own language to create a clear vision of the athletic performance you *do* want. Simply ask yourself the question: ***What is a short phrase that clearly and precisely states the performance I do want?*** For example: To reach a recent personal weightlifting goal, I used the positive performance phrase: *I have the heavy lifting foundation under me. I am ready to make this lift.*

- Practice keeping your mental focus on how you *do* want to play, never on how you don't want to play. If you catch yourself falling back into *I don't...* thinking, you can instantly make the shift back to how you do want to play; practice staying in this *do* zone. For example: It's game time and, in a key moment, a pitcher catches the thought *don't give up a home run* and instantly, before throwing the next pitch, shift to *I'm going after this hitter!*

- If you keep getting performances you don't want, check to see if—when you tell yourself the truth—you have your mental focus on what you don't want to have happen.

STEP 5: VIVIDLY VISUALIZE YOUR DO-WANT PERFORMANCE

- Practice thinking, saying, seeing, hearing and feeling your positive-performance phrase. Rather than leaving you feeling stressed out and hesitant, your chosen positive-performance phrase should relax your body and calm your mind.
- Keep in mind that champions keep their mental focus on what they do during their top performances, not on their mistakes.
- Watch for negativity lurking behind your attempted positivity.

Watch for these potential trouble spots during your Step 5 practice:

- Are you thinking and saying your positive-performance phrase with no feeling? Just saying the words isn't enough—fill your whole mind and body with the experience. If it doesn't stir up positive, excited feelings for you, rework it until it does.
- Positive-phrase practice must be free of "buts." Whatever you think and say after the word *but* is what your mind/body focuses on. For example, a positive-performance phrase is negated if you say: *I'm ready to hit, but I haven't ever hit well off this pitcher* or *I'm ready to hit, but I haven't ever hit well in this ballpark.* Subconscious thoughts

like these wipe out your conscious efforts to truly be positive and ready for the next performance moment. Stick with *I'm ready to hit* and get ready to drive the ball into a gap.

STEP 6: LOCK IN THE SHIFT IN SELF-BELIEFS

- Use your mental ability to **detach** from old, negative self-beliefs. You are not your thoughts; the negative thinking is just an idea in your mind. Let it go—it's not who you really are, nor does it reflect your true athletic ability! For example, one Division I college golfer I worked with had just shot the third lowest 54-hole score in her school's history. As the next tournament was coming up, she caught the thought, *I don't know if I belong on top the leader board*. As you build a stronger mental game, you will begin breaking through past performance barriers and start playing to your potential. At this point, it is critical that you catch any old thought/belief like the one noted above which can sabotage your progress.

- The golfer mentioned above began to think and believe, based now on her results, *I do belong!* To let it go, shift to a more positive identity by practicing words and thoughts like these: *It is the old me who used to be negative about my abilities anytime things went wrong.* ***The new me is now able to keep my eye solely on how***

I do want to perform and on my true athletic ability.

STEP 7: PRACTICE, PRACTICE, PRACTICE!

- Put significant effort into practicing your mental and emotional self-management skills. Although people in athletics are very clear about the value of diligently practicing physical skills, they are are much less clear about the value of practicing mental and emotional self-management skills. Don't take my word for it. Prove to yourself that diligently practicing a mental-game system will really pay off!

- Decide to be determined and faithfully practice your mental-game skills. Stick with it! It is building a strong mental-game system and mastering the skills through practice that helps you quickly bounce back from poor-performance moments to become a consistent top performer.

- Remember that you are now learning what to do when things don't go your way. No more coping and waiting, wishing, and hoping that the bad times will go away by themselves just because you're no longer consciously aware of the upset. The down moments will never have the same grip on you because now, when you have a moment of not playing like you want, you can remember: *I know what to do now to mentally and emotionally self-manage this poor-performance moment.*

Add These Key Practices for a Performance Boost

- **Stay and play in the present moment.** A quick trick to get back into the present moment when you catch yourself focused on something in the past or future is to think and say: *Now is how!*
- **Breathe the right way.** True relaxation requires slow, abdominal breathing. Place your hand on your stomach and feel/watch your hand ***move out when you inhale and in when you exhale***. It pays to check your breathing, because many athletes who habitually take a breath during performance moments often breathe shallowly in the chest—or even backwards.
- **"Read" your body posture** moment by moment. Physical motion creates different emotion. Slumping, slouching posture keeps you negative for as long as you hold that posture. You can quickly get rid of negativity by moving your body

back into proud, confident posture no matter how things are going.

- **Practice self-responsibility**. Look inside and admit the troubling situations you are responsible for. Truly decide that you will spend no more time blaming others for the way your sports life is going.

- **Practice self-acceptance.** It is only when you accept yourself just as you are that you can begin to change. Accepting a situation doesn't have to mean you agree with it, it simply means you tell yourself the truth; admit that it has happened.

- **Admit and allow your true feelings**, instead of trying to block them out. Feel the feelings, don't fight the feelings. For example, if you are frustrated or mad, admit it. Notice where you feel that upset energy in your body, and then imagine it moving out of your mind and body. Michelle, a protégé, aptly wrote: "The most impressive piece of information for me was to acknowledge your true feelings and tap on them. This helped me a lot yesterday, before a competition and also made me realize why I had blanked several times in my previous comp, as I had been telling myself I wasn't nervous—be positive, etc., keeping the feelings down. Then they suddenly take over in the middle of the comp with no warning! It's great to think I can now stop this from happening again."

- **Watch your word choices**. Build a championship vocabulary! We think in words, and our brain runs our body, so become aware of the words you put in your brain. Words affect how we play. For example: the simple words *don't* and *slump* always mess up sport performance because they keep you focused on what's going wrong instead of what you want to do right. Practice catching any other negative word habits and shift to an inspiring, positive word.

- **Watch the questions you ask**, because the instant you ask a question, your mind focuses on answering the question. For example, if you ask lousy questions like *Why do I keep hitting right at people?* or *Why can't I get ahead of hitters?* your mind will work to answer and your mind will stay focused on how you *don't* want to play. Instead, ask positive, quality questions like ***What is one thing I can start doing right away to start hitting in the gaps?*** or ***What is one thing I can do right now to start getting ahead of hitters?***

Have you noticed yet what your thoughts and feelings are doing to you physically?

Has anyone ever taught you that you can work with the natural energy flowing in your body?

Do you know that sport performance mental training practitioners now have a great method for clearing emotional upset out of your system once and for all?

Are you aware that a single thought can knock out your ability to physically perform the physical skills of your sport?

The next section explains how thinking and feeling habits can affect your sport performance, and teaches what to do about them. You're about to learn how to use a dependable tool that will relax your body and calm your mind during practices and game-time. You can count on it!

Emotional Freedom Techniques (EFT)

POOR PERFORMANCES HAVE more to do with blocked energy in your body than with lack of will power. Your thoughts turn into energy that goes into the cells of your whole body and affect your physical performance.

Energy psychology encompasses several innovative stress-management tools that combine the latest knowledge from the mental health field with knowledge of the ancient acupuncture meridian system to manage the natural energy flows in your body. These dependable methods help you quickly achieve a relaxed body and calm mind by activating natural acupuncture points on your body. One specific energy psychology method is called EFT, a self-help method developed by Gary Craig. I have taught my modified version of EFT for well over a decade.

With this method, you will physically tap certain

energy points on your body while tuning your mind into your current thoughts and feelings. Struggling with trying to analyze and out-think the performance problem is over. Instead, tapping on these natural energy (acupuncture) points will quickly relax your body and clear your mind, putting yourself in the ideal performance state.

Athletes tell me they really like this tool for clearing bad-performance moments out of their mind and body because it gives them something specific they can do *right now*. One top college pitcher said, *I wanted something tangible like EFT so that I no longer have to fight thoughts in my head.*

EFT is the fastest, most effective, and most dependable method available for flushing upset emotional energy out of your mind and body!

How to Tap

THE PURPOSE OF tapping is to activate your ener-gy system to clear out mental/emotional blocks. Use your index and middle fingertips on each hand and tap (seven times or so) on the illustrated points (see pages 34 and 35 for diagrams). Tap hard enough to hear it, but not so hard it hurts.

The number of times you tap each point does not have to be exact, it can be more than seven or less—whatever begins to feel right to you.

All of the points, except the two points near your lips and the point on your sternum, are bilateral—the points are on both sides of your body—so you can tap one side or both sides. I prefer to tap all points, both sides, because once you know the points, it takes about one minute to tap on all of them and athletes are often unaware of where the mental and emotional blocks are in their body. When you tap all of the points you will be activating the energy flow in all 14 of the energy lines (a microtubule, like a small vein or artery) in your body, in effect "talking" to, and effectively clearing, your whole mind/body system of any unnoticed upset.

Alternatives to Tapping

I LIKE THE EFT tapping method, but I have learned that tapping will never be for everybody. Some athletes I work with tell me they want something they can actually *do* to relax, but they ask for techniques that are less noticeable than tapping during game time.

The important thing with this method is to stir up the natural energy flows in your body to keep your body's energy lines clear of upset emotional interference. You can activate your natural energy flows in one of three ways and you can test drive them to discover what works best for you. You can:

1. **Tap:** Physically tap the energy points using your index and middle finger on each hand. This is the method created by Gary Craig called EFT.
2. **Touch:** Touch the energy points by holding your index and middle fingertips on each point long enough to take a normal breath (inhaling and exhaling) before moving to the next point. This

method comes from another energy psychology system called Touch and Breathe (TAB), created by John Diepold, Ph.D.

3. **Massage:** You can simply massage each identified energy point with your fingertips, a technique used in acupressure.

If you choose to use the tapping or massaging methods, practice "reading" your body to determine how firmly or softly, quickly or slowly, gently or vigor-ously the movement should be to activate your energy points. Practice different ways to learn what works best for you.

When to Tap

THE "RIGHT" ISSUES to tap on will be revealed through diligently practicing self-honest self-observation. This is where the cognitive practices in the *Step-by-Step* section tie together with the body-energy based techniques described in this energy psychology section.

Keep it simple and just tap for what is happening in the moment. Activate the energy points for any thoughts and/or feelings and sensations in your body you want to release, such as tight shoulders, butterflies in your stomach, rapid breathing, shaking hands, self-doubt, anger, frustration, and so forth. Admit and allow the upsetting thought and feeling while you are tapping which is the technique for totally clearing it out of your system; instead of fighting, denying or skipping past the upset to try and get positive. (See p. 12, **Admit and allow your true feelings,** for detail.)

You can also tap to lock in your positive-performance phrase. Tap the energy points while mentally focusing on your phrase. For example: *I choose to see, feel, and remember in my whole mind and body throwing strikes and getting ground ball outs,* which is a phrase one top pitcher successfully used when he pitched and won 4 post-season games and helped his team win the 2012 Division I College World Series.

How to Use the Method

TO CLEAR NEGATIVITY out of your mind-body system, turn your mental focus to a troubling thought, feeling, or behavior that is happening right now. Work with only *one* thought or emotion at a time. Be specific and tell yourself the truth. Focus on what is happening *in the moment* while describing the issue in your own words.

With your mind tuned in, begin tapping the acupuncture points (illustrated on pages 34–35) on the 14 main energy lines to "stir up," or get your body's natural energy flowing. When you start tapping the points, work to keenly notice your mind-body experiences throughout the round of tapping.

As an example of how this works, let's take a close look at one athlete's experience. Anthony, a Division I college baseball player, told me he was experiencing the "yips" in his throws back to the pitcher. First, remember the key practice of catching your word choices: it's best to eliminate the word "yips" from your vocabulary and call it something like "a temporary throwing issue" or "temporary throwing trouble." Anthony couldn't get this throwing trouble resolved and couldn't, no matter how hard he tried, put the trouble out of his mind. Anthony agreed that he couldn't fix the throwing trouble by ignoring it, so he practiced self-honesty and allowed himself to catch the thought and feel the feelings related to the throwing trouble. While tapping, he used the thought and feeling statement *I have a throwing issue and it really makes me mad.*

You can repeat your phrase silently in your mind or out loud; I've observed that saying it out loud is most effective for maintaining focus. Scott, a Division I college baseball pitcher, gave up a home run and his team lost; it was a key loss because the team was working to be selected for post-season play. He still had this troubling performance moment on his mind and the upset emotional energy in his body even though it was ten days later. I asked Scott to describe, in his own words, what he was still thinking and feeling about that moment. His script, in his own words, for tapping the energy points was:

- Tap the eyebrow point while saying *frustration toward myself.*
- Tap the side of the eye point while saying *frustration toward myself.*
- Tap under the eye while saying *frustration toward myself.*

- Tap under the nose while saying *frustration toward myself.*
- Tap under the mouth while saying *frustration toward myself*

…and so forth through the rest of the energy points on upper torso and hands.

As frequently happens in tapping the energy points to clear out blocked emotional energy, Scott and Anthony noticed a mental shift. Anthony said he noticed new awareness: *I feel like the tension is leaving my arms and hands and I am getting to a clear mind more quickly.*

The 9-Gamut Series

The EFT system originally included the 9-Gamut series, a key practice that is very useful for relieving anxiety, stress, and worry. It was a series of eye motions, humming, and counting while tapping continuously on the back-of-the-hand point. I continue to use and teach it. In his book, *Tapping the Healer Within,* Dr. Roger Callahan called this the "gamut series" because it encompasses a wide range of treatments. To use the gamut series, use the steps on the following page while focusing on the issue and continuously tapping the back-of-the-hand point:

1. Close your eyes for a moment.
2. Open your eyes.

Then, with your eyes open and head still:

3. Look down to the right.
4. Look down to the left.
5. Roll your eyes in a full circle one way.
6. Roll your eyes in a full circle the other way.
7. Hum a favorite tune (activating the creative/emotional right side of your brain).
8. Count to 7 (activating the logic, reasoning and problem-solving left side of your brain).
9. Finish with humming a favorite tune.

Even though this process may seem silly and unnecessary, there is evidence that it balances your brain activity so it works efficiently for the physical skills you must perform in your sport. And remember: your brain runs your body.

To get a better sense of your progress with clearing sports performance upset out of your mind-body, it can help to use a 0-to-10 scale, where 0 means the issue is gone and 10 means it is still strongly interfering. Start the tapping process by giving a number rating for how much of a problem this seems to be for you. Then after each round of tapping, re-rate the issue using the 10-point scale. One sign that you have cleared your mind/body system of the upset emotional energy is that you can think of the problem again and you rate yourself at a 1 or 0.

Boost your effectiveness in clearing emotional upset out of your system by saying to yourself, after each round of tapping, **When I tell myself the truth**, *I'm still mad at myself* or **When I tell myself the truth**, *after this first round of tapping, I'm still a little nervous about next week's game.* Sometimes you get a clear sense of freedom from the stress-producing issue in one round of tapping the energy points, and sometimes it can take multiple rounds.

The Final Step
The final step in the EFT system is to continuously tap the side-of-the-hand point and say the words *even though....* followed by a description of the situation you are experiencing and then state the truth of your situation. For example, Anthony said some version of the statement below three times:

> **Even though** I have this throwing issue and
> it really makes me mad, **the truth is** that this
> is what I am feeling for now **and I totally
> and completely accept myself** and my body
> anyway.

Once again, I coached Anthony to fully feel, as much as possible, the emotional experience that this anger (in essence, worry and stress) brings up while also noticing the experience throughout his mind and body. Anthony clarified this when he stated, "you mean engage with the feelings" and I agreed that he, in his own words, had re-stated this key point accurately.

This final step helps you achieve a state of self-acceptance. When working toward self-acceptance, always **choose language that states the temporary nature** of any performance trouble spot. Nothing lasts forever, even though sometimes it can feel that way. Remember, self-acceptance doesn't mean you like what happened, it simply means you admit to yourself what happened. As always, use the words and phrases that have meaning to you.

Sometimes a person isn't comfortable with the phrase *totally and completely accept myself*, so if you tell yourself the truth and that is true for you, you can back up a step and use language like this: *I **am willing** to start accepting myself about this situation/trouble spot in my performance….*

You will notice in the example, I used the phrase, *accept myself and my body*. Athletes often unconsciously get mad at their bodies when their bodies don't do what they have rigorously trained them to do. In this case, you would say *Even though (insert the issue here), I totally accept myself **and my body**.* And, finally, it can help you move toward self-acceptance when you put the word *anyway* at the end of your self-acceptance statement: *Even though (insert the issue here), I totally accept myself and my body anyway.*

What to Do While Tapping

TO BEGIN, TURN your mental focus to *one* troubling thought, feeling, or behavior that is happening right now. Tell yourself the truth and describe the thought or emotion in your own words, and *be specific*.

With your mind tuned in, begin tapping the energy points to "stir up" your body's natural energy flows always intending to feel relaxed. The effectiveness of the tapping is improved when you set a goal to end up feeling relaxed after each round of tapping. Work to keenly notice your mind-body experiences throughout each round of tapping. You are practicing reading your body for any remaining tension.

Where to Tap

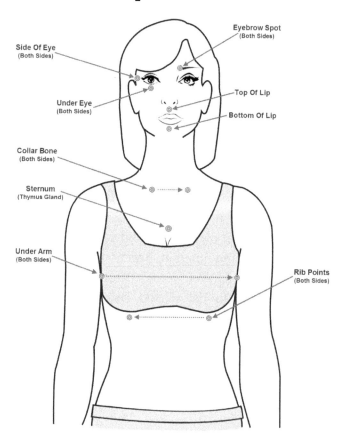

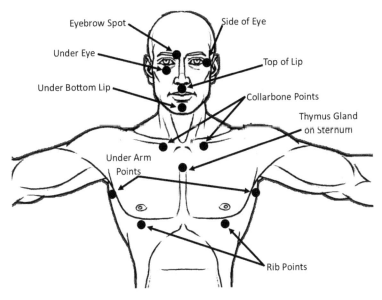

Eyebrow Spot

Side of Eye

Under Eye

Top of Lip

Under Bottom Lip

Collarbone Points

Thymus Gland on Sternum

Under Arm Points

Rib Points

Note: I have included a male and female image to honor all athletes. The points utilized, though, are the same. All of the points, except the top lip, bottom lip and the sternum point, are bilateral. The points are on both sides of your body, so you can tap one side or both. Again, I usually tap all of the points, both sides, because the identified points activate the energy flow in all 14 energy lines (meridians) running throughout your body/mind. Once you know the points it only takes about one minute. Plus, we often don't know, or are not consciously aware of, where the trapped emotional upset resides in our body, so tapping all of the points can help you clear out all upset.

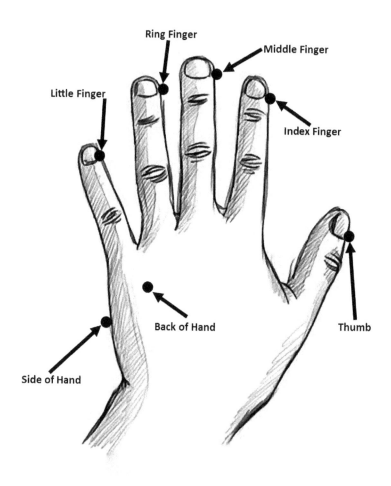

Key Point: It is most efficient to tap each hand point right beside the fingernail because that is the end of the energy (meridian) line and there is less electrical resistance.

Note: You can tap one hand only or the points on both hands.

The Three-Minute Routine

I RECOMMEND USING this Three-Minute Routine as a fast and effective body-energy warm-up before workouts, practices, and games. The three steps in the routine are intended to assist you with achieving peak coordination, balance, and mental clarity.

As you begin practicing with this routine, start by focusing on how your body feels *right now* and what is on your mind, and then proceed to go through the three steps. Afterward, take a moment to notice how your mind and body feel.

Minutes 1 and 2: Center and balance your energy flow

For your mind-body to function optimally, you want energy efficiently crossing over the mid-line of your body, with the right side of the brain sending energy messages to the left side of your body, and the left side of the brain sending messages to the right side of your body. The Hook-up and Cross Crawl accomplish this energy rewiring for you, helping you to achieve peak coordination, balance, and a clear mind.

You can perform the hook-up lying down, sitting down or standing up. Some athletes tell me they are using the hook up while lying in bed to aid their sleep.

The Hook-up (1 minute)

1. Cross your ankles and extend your arms out in front of you, putting the opposite wrist on top (that is, opposite from whichever ankle is on top).

2. Roll your hands over each other so your palms are touching and interlock your fingers, then pull your intertwined hands down and under, against your chest.

3. While holding this position, breath in through your nose and out through your mouth, intending to feel centered and balanced. You can visualize the balance or sense it.

The Cross Crawl (1 minute)

1. While standing or sitting, bend your left knee and raise your leg, moving your knee across the mid-line of your body. Touch your right elbow to your left knee.

2. Switch sides, bending your right knee and touching it with your left elbow.

3. Repeat Steps 1 and 2 about 10 or 15 times, moving easily while your body loosens up. You can perform this energy warm up standing up or sitting down.

Minute 3: Do at least one round of EFT tapping

During this last step of the 3-Minute Routine, you can tap for any specific thought, feeling, or performance issue. If your preparation is going fine and you have no specific personal focus for the round of tapping as you get ready for a game, consider using the following protocol:

Think about (or, ideally, say out loud) and feel (in your body) each phrase listed below and move to a different energy point for each line. There is no perfect way to use this protocol, just follow the general instructions and make it work for you. Start your tapping with the eyebrow point while saying the first line, shift to the side of eye point while saying the second line, and so on, moving to a new energy point for each line of the protocol.

*I'm letting go of all **noticed and unnoticed** tension in my mind and body, joints and muscles.*

*I'm letting go of all **noticed and unnoticed** negative-thought energy right now.*

*I'm letting go of all **noticed and unnoticed** doubt about my upcoming performance.*

I'm choosing to transform this energy into a powerful performance.

I'm choosing to create a laser-like focus on my true athletic ability.

I'm choosing to feel calm, energetic, and focused.

I'm choosing to easily move into the flow of my game/run/workout.

I'm choosing to enjoy the game/run/workout.

I'm choosing to let it be easy and fun!

In these affirmations, *easy* means *effortless*, not being lazy or showing lack of effort.

Choose words that have meaning to you; any words I offer are suggestions only and can be changed.

You can use this three-minute routine before practice and before the game as a super preparation ritual: it's a body energy warm up that you won't achieve with thinking only.

As a quick system shortcut, try the acronym WAC:

Try the acronym WAC as a shortcut way to remember the system:

    W *atch (the current thought/feeling)*
    A *llow (the current thought/feeling)*
    C *lear out (with EFT)*

What Can EFT Be Used For

ALTHOUGH EFT IS still new to the sports world, it is gaining ground due to its dependability and effectiveness. It's pain-free, side effect-free, and uses the natural energy already in your body. So you can try it for anything and everything!

EFT TAPPING CAN BE EFFECTIVE IN SPORT PERFORMANCE BECAUSE YOU WILL:

- Address mental/emotional blocks to peak performance;
- Instantly boost your energy;
- Recover more rapidly from practice efforts and game performances;
- Reduce fatigue in general;
- Recover more rapidly from physical injury;
- Improve workout performances and break through training plateaus;
- Move past your comfort zones;

- Increase your physical range of motion;
- Implement mechanical changes more rapidly (e.g., changes in swing, pitching form, and so forth);
- Enhance sleep and relaxation;
- Enhance sustained attention on academic work;
- Manage adjusting to travel issues (e.g., jet lag, changes in times zones, environment, new ball-parks, weather, and so forth); and
- Much more...

To illustrate how to use language to address any of the sports performance areas noted above read the following example:

I choose to quickly and easily adjust in my whole mind and body to _____ e.g. this trip, change in ball park, weather, pitching mound, etc. You can fill in the blank and use the tapping points to stay mentally and emotionally calm about any changes and/or adjustments you are making with your sport.

For more rapid recovery from workouts and during and after games, you can focus and say: *I choose to quickly and easily recover in my whole mind and body* (or focus on specific body parts that seem particularly tired or sore) *from this workout/the last inning/this game.*

Putting It All Together

IN A NUTSHELL, put your total attention on your mind and body. Become aware of whether you feel stressed and hesitant or relaxed and ready. Use these feelings and sensations as your inner guide to knowing whether or not you are mentally and physically ready to play your sport. If you notice stress, tap for whatever is on your mind and in your body.

Diligently practice self-honest self-observation by watching your thoughts and feelings and telling yourself the truth about what you notice, without getting mad at yourself for what you see. Develop an attitude of mastering your mental-game skills, just as you do with your physical skills.

If, when you tell yourself the truth, you notice stress, start with **allowing** any negativity to come into your awareness and clear that out of your mind and body first. Tune your mind to those issues and tap the energy points to clear them out.

Check in with yourself and if you still notice the negativity, do another round of tapping.

Continue rounds of tapping until you can think about the issue you were tapping for without getting upset or until a new thought pops into your mind.

Finish with a round of tapping, putting your attention this time on how you *do* want to perform. Tap a round while thinking and saying, *I choose to quickly and easily (insert your positive performance phrase). I'm focusing my whole mind and body on how I do want to play my sport.*

All the best to you as you move forward in your sport!

Greg Warburton

FOR MORE INFORMATION

YOU'RE WARMLY INVITED to contact me directly to learn more about Warburton's Winning System or talk to me about one-on-one or team coaching:
Greg Warburton
Sport Performance Mental Training Coach
Licensed Professional Counselor
CEO, Inner Liberty, Inc.
Web: **gregwarburton.com**
Email: *greg@gregwarburton.com*
Phone: **541-971-9810** (call or text)
Skype: greg.warburton1

GET THE MAIN BOOK

Want a copy of my main book which explains and illustrates my system in much more detail, ***Warburton's Winning System: Tapping and Other Transformational Mental Training Tools***? Visit my website, or log on to Amazon or your favorite book-buying

site, or my author's page: www.outskirtspress.com/
warburtonswinningsystem.

LIVE RECORDINGS AVAILABLE

To hear me talk on the radio and in teleconference
about mental and emotional self-management skills
training, see: my website and/or **youtube.com/user/
gregwarburton**.

ESPECIALLY FOR COACHES

I would jump at the chance to introduce Warburton's
Winning System to your team and put you on the road
to a championship season. My intention is not to re-
place anyone or anything you already have in place.
I want to boost your coaching effectiveness by adding
mental-training tools to assist your players with quickly
developing mental and emotional self-management
skills and, ultimately, giving your team that championship edge. Just email me, and I'll apply a group discount
to my mental-training coaching services and books.

BEYOND SPORTS

Although this book applies Warburton's Winning
System to sports, these powerful techniques can be
used to handle any aspect of life, both on and off the
field. When you visit my website, be sure to access
these complimentary articles:

- *Why Thoughts Really Matter in Sports,
  Academics and Life*

- *The Power of Praise Revisited: A Full Formula*
- *The Building Blocks for Banishing Bad Habits*

JOIN THE COMMUNITY

These simple, effective, life-changing skills are not taught in any schools, nor are they taught on the athletic field so please join me in teaching them to as many coaches, parents, and young people as you possibly can. Here are three ways you can help spread the word:

1. Send friends to my website.
2. Purchase gift copies of this book and/or the main book, **Warburton's Winning System**, for friends, family, loved ones, and business associates.
3. Spread the word through your social media accounts.

CPSIA information can be obtained
at www.ICGtesting.com
Printed in the USA
BVHW01s1039081217
502256BV00014B/177/P